Struggle for Justice

Struggle for Justice

◆

The Story of Dr. Wan Azizah Wan Ismail of Malaysia

Hiroko Iwami Malott

iUniverse, Inc.
New York Lincoln Shanghai

Struggle for Justice
The Story of Dr. Wan Azizah Wan Ismail of Malaysia

iUniverse books may be ordered through booksellers or by contacting:

iUniverse
2021 Pine Lake Road, Suite 100
Lincoln, NE 68512
www.iuniverse.com
1-800-Authors (1-800-288-4677)

ISBN-13: 978-0-595-37586-8 (pbk)
ISBN-13: 978-0-595-81981-2 (ebk)
ISBN-10: 0-595-37586-3 (pbk)
ISBN-10: 0-595-81981-8 (ebk)

Printed in the United States of America

For my Mother, Setsuko Iwami

And in memory of my Father,

General Takeshi Iwami

Contents

Struggle for Justice

(Left to Right) The author, Hiroko Iwami Malott; Nurul Izzah, the eldest daughter of Anwar Ibrahim and Dr. Wan Azizah; and Datin Seri Dr. Wan Azizah Wan Ismail. Photograph taken at the United States Ambassador's Residence in Kuala Lumpur, Malaysia, November 1998

Preface to the 2005 English Edition

In 2000, Ms. Miyuki Suzuki of Tokyo asked me to write a story for her Japanese language website, *La Vie en Rose*.

Ms. Suzuki introduced me to her readers this way:

> "As the wife of an American diplomat for many years, Hiroko Malott has taken many impressionable journeys in wartime Vietnam, India, and Malaysia, and that is why we asked her to tell us what she saw and felt during that time."

Ms. Suzuki gave me my choice of what to write about, and I chose to tell the story of my friend, Dr. Wan Azizah Wan Ismail, the wife of the former Deputy Prime Minister and Finance Minister of Malaysia, Anwar Ibrahim. There was no story that I wanted to tell more.

In 1998, while my husband was serving as the United States Ambassador, Malaysia's political situation turned into a crisis. In September of that year Anwar Ibrahim, who was the Deputy Prime Minister and Finance Minister, was ousted from his position and arrested on the orders of Prime Minister Mahathir Mohamed. Anwar's struggle attracted the attention of the world.

I was an eyewitness to those developments and knew many of the players personally. I counted Azizah among my friends in Malaysia.

The events of 1998 heralded a new phase in Malaysia's political history that continues to this day.

The developments of the past six years have been chronicled by many, but almost all accounts have Anwar as the central character.

The story I told on the internet was different, because I wrote from the perspective not of Anwar but of his wife Azizah. It is the story of a woman, written by a woman.

This is the story of a woman whose entire life changed on one fateful night in September 1998.

This story was written originally for a Japanese audience, because I believed that it was important for the Japanese people—and especially Japanese women—to know the truth about what is happening in Malaysia. I wanted them to know about Anwar and Azizah, who became the living symbol of the movement for greater democracy, justice, and freedom in Malaysia.

After my story appeared on *La Vie en Rose's* website, I printed a number of copies of the Japanese text to give to friends in Japan. But there were many friends in America who wanted to read it, too. So with my husband's assistance, we translated it into English and passed out dozens and dozens of copies.

But Azizah's struggle for justice continued, even after 2000, so I kept adding updates. Now that the story has concluded with a happy ending, I have updated it again.

As you read this book, the first twelve chapters are based on the original Japanese website story. The final two chapters carry the story forward from the year 2000.

As this story of Azizah is published formally, there are many people whom I would like to thank, starting with Ms. Miyuki Suzuki, who encouraged me to write it, and my husband John, who helped translated it into English.

I also would like to thank Raja Petra Raja Kamaruddin of the Free Anwar Campaign for his encouragement, and for allowing me to use the Campaign's photographs of Anwar and Azizah in this book.

But most of all I would like to thank Azizah and her wonderful family. Over the past six years, despite being half a world away, she has become one of my very best friends. It has been my honor to tell her story.

Alexandria, Virginia
October 2005

Preface to the
2000 Japanese Internet Edition

My name is Hiroko Malott. I am Japanese, but I am also an American citizen.

It has been 28 years since I married an American diplomat, John Malott. It has been one and a half years since we left our final diplomatic post, Malaysia.

From wartime Vietnam to Malaysia, countries in political crisis, my everyday life was tied together with American diplomacy.

After nearly three decades in diplomatic life, there are many stories I could tell about the different places and people I came to know, and the events I witnessed firsthand.

But more than anyone else, it is Datin Seri Dr. Wan Azizah Wan Ismail, the wife of Anwar Ibrahim, the former Deputy Prime Minister of Malaysia, whom I would like to tell you about.

Today Azizah is the leader of Malaysia's Justice Party (Keadilan), and one of the leaders of the political opposition in Malaysia.

During my three years in Malaysia, neither Azizah nor I ever could have imagined the situation that she would be in today. Those seemed such wonderful times. But then in 1998 her world—and Malaysia's world—turned upside down.

The day before I left Malaysia in December 1998, I went to say farewell. On that day, Azizah's husband Anwar Ibrahim, the former Deputy Prime Minister of Malaysia, was in jail, and that is where he still is today.

When I saw Azizah, I asked her what I could do. She said, "I hope that somehow the people of Japan can hear more about our struggle."

Why Japan? During my three years in Malaysia, the Malaysian people always saw me in an interesting way.

I was the wife of the American Ambassador, but they also saw me as an Asian and a Japanese, someone from a country for which they had great respect. Japan was a non-Western country that had achieved great success. It seemed that many Malaysians somehow felt closer to me because I was Japanese.

Since that time, I have been searching for an opportunity to carry out my promise to tell Azizah's story to the people of Japan, and indeed, the whole world.

Malaysia's leaders claim that they are a democracy and that their people have freedom of speech, but I know that is not so. I lived there for three years, and I have watched what has happened since. Anwar's wife and family do not have the freedom to say what they would like. That is the situation they are in.

So I decided, I can say what they cannot. That is what I can do. Because I am an American—and a Japanese—and because I live in a free country, with freedom of speech and a free press, I can tell you what I saw. I can help you come to know about this wonderful woman, Dr. Wan Azizah, and her struggle for justice.

And I can let you read Azizah's own words, words that never have appeared in the press in her own country. Words from her interviews, from her conversations with me, and words that she has written especially for our Japanese readers.

I love Malaysia and the Malaysian people. My husband and I often talk about how nice it would be to travel back and forth between Malaysia and America, and even live in both countries in the future.

But I also love freedom.

I hope for the day when all Malaysians can live in a country where they are truly free to say, write, and think what they want, when men like Anwar Ibrahim are not put in jail for daring to criticize the leader of the Government, and when wonderful women like Wan Azizah and her family are not deprived of their husbands and fathers and threatened with arrest.

That is the kind of country we Japanese live in.

That is the kind of country I know the people of Malaysia want to live in.

That is the kind of world that we all want to live in.

Laguna Niguel, California
2000

1

September 20, 1998
Kuala Lumpur

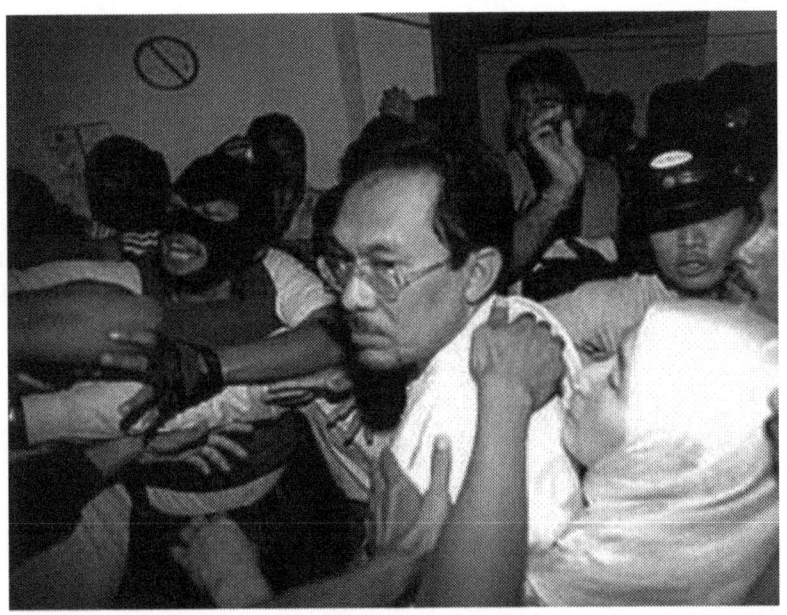

Anwar is arrested, as Azizah holds on to him

SEPTEMBER 20, 1998
KUALA LUMPUR

One night, suddenly and without warning, a special SWAT Team carrying automatic weapons smashes down the door to your home, and without saying anything, they arrest your husband and take him away.

What would *you* do?

Your children are crying as these masked men point their weapons at you.

Your husband is arrested under something called the Internal Security Act, an act that the colonial British government used to fight against communist guerrillas in Malaya decades before. But your husband is not a communist, and he has never taken up arms against the government.

This Internal Security Act (ISA) pays no heed to the rights of your husband. Under the ISA, your husband is not allowed to see his lawyers, and he will not be subject to normal court proceedings. You are not allowed to visit your husband, and you have no way of knowing whether he is safe or not.

You don't even know whether he is alive.

What is going on?

This would be a frightening situation for anyone.

But you are not just anyone.

Your husband, Anwar Ibrahim, has been the Deputy Prime Minister of Malaysia. He has been the second most powerful man in the country. Everyone thought that one day he would become the Prime Minister.

And now, on September 20, 1998, he has been taken away from you at gunpoint, before your eyes and the eyes of your children, in your home, in a shocking and brutal arrest.

And on that day, your struggle for justice began.

Azizah described what happened this way:

> "At that time, Anwar was holding a press conference. There were many
> foreign correspondents and Malaysian supporters gathered there. There
> were about 100 ordinary police with rifles surrounding the house. Then
> suddenly a SWAT team with rifles broke into the house and kicked
> down the door.[1] There was shouting and confusion everywhere, and
> then they pointed a gun at Anwar. They put him into the police car to
> take him away.
>
> "I thought I needed to follow after my husband. So the children and I
> got into the vehicle. But in the confusion our youngest daughter Hana
> was not with us. She ran after us, crying, "Papa! Papa!" I could see her in
> the darkness, her crying face lit by the taillights. Hana was only six then.
> From that day she developed a high fever and had to be hospitalized,
> although now she is at home with us."

That's the way Azizah described the worst night of her life—with her usual
soft voice.

At that time, I was the wife of the U.S. Ambassador to Malaysia. We heard the
same story about the arrest. The press was there as Anwar was arrested. When little Hana was left behind, they rushed to take pictures of her, standing in the
street alone, frightened and crying.

Malaysia's three television stations did not report much on Anwar's arrest, so
people could only learn the news by watching the international satellite channels,
CNN and CNBC. But there were no pictures on CNN of little Hana running
after the car with her mother in it. The police confiscated the foreign cameramen's film and tapes. That was a picture the Malaysian Government did not
want the world to see.

A few days after this happened, my husband and I went to call on Azizah. We
went as her friends. The situation in Malaysia was tense, and most of her friends,

---

1.   Azizah later told me that people were coming in and out of the house all night, and
      the door was unlocked. But still the police smashed down an unlocked door and
      broke the windowpane!

for understandable reasons, were afraid to go to see her. But we were different. My husband was the American Ambassador, and the Government and police could not stop us from going.

When we arrived at her house, we saw the hole in the front door where the police had smashed it in, and the windowpane that they knocked out. It made everything seem so real as we thought about what had happened to Anwar and his family in that very room.

Yet the house was very calm. We sat on a simple couch in a room that had a cabinet but not much more. There was a picture of Anwar on the wall.

During our years in Malaysia, we had visited many houses of the "rich and famous." But compared to the rich and elegant homes of other Cabinet Ministers whom we had visited, Anwar's house was rather modest.

Within days after Anwar's arrest, we had heard the same rumors that Azizah had heard: that Anwar had been beaten, that he was in a coma, and even that he had been killed. It was hard to believe. Only a month before, her husband was the country's Deputy Prime Minister, and people would rush to be close to her and her husband. And now she heard these stories but was unable to learn anything about his condition.

Anwar was expected by everyone to be Prime Minister Mahathir's successor. His popularity and political power were on the rise. Everyone thought that the day was approaching when Mahathir would turn over the Prime Minister's chair to Anwar. Even Mahathir said that he would do so.

And it wasn't just in Malaysia. Overseas as well, Anwar was seen as one of Asia's new leaders. With my own eyes I saw how many politicians and businessmen, from both Malaysia and overseas, wanted to be close to Anwar.

Now, with his arrest, all of that changed.

As I spoke to Azizah that day, one of her young daughters peeked around the door.

Azizah has six children, the oldest being 19, and I had brought a present for each of them that I hoped would fit each one personally. So that's why she was peeking—she wanted to come and say thank you.

> "Auntie, thank you for the present. Hana is in bed, but she wants me to say thank you for her, too." And then she said, "But is it okay for us to accept this?" She smiled at her mother, who smiled back with a signal that it was okay, and she dashed off to open the gift!

And I thought it was only days before that her father was taken away at gunpoint, and my heart filled with pain.

I visited the house by myself a few times after that. Once I brought some used movie videotapes for the children to watch. I knew that the children could not go out much after their father was arrested. It wasn't just ostracism and what others would say to them; there were rumors that they would be kidnapped.

When I brought the videotapes, Azizah's son Ihsan picked up one of them—I think it was "Zorro"—and he said, "I always wanted to watch this movie. But is it all right for us to accept this many tapes?" More than anything else, what I remember is how cheerful those children were, how well-mannered, and how strong they were, considering everything that had happened. It was clear that the love of their father and mother had made this a strong family and bound them together.

And one more thing. I know children well, as a mother. After Anwar was arrested, his political enemies tried to accuse him of corruption. But children are the most honest people on earth. If Anwar's children were accustomed to receiving presents, and if they lived in a home where presents would suddenly appear everyday, they would not have asked permission to take even a videotape or a small doll.

After my husband and I left Azizah's house on that first visit, a number of men came rushing up to us. Some had video cameras pointing at us. One of them asked my husband, "Mr. Ambassador, what are you doing here?" And my husband replied, "This was a personal visit."

That's all he said, and he got into the car—which, by the way was not his official car with the American flag on it, but our personal vehicle—a Toyota Camry. That was to emphasize that this was a private visit.

Then they came after me and pointed a microphone and asked the same question. I replied, "Azizah is my friend, so I came to see her."

After we got home, we learned that even as we were talking to Azizah the charges against Anwar had been changed from a violation of the Internal Security Act to criminal charges, and that he had been transferred to a regular jail. In a way, this was good news—it meant that now Anwar would have a right to see his lawyers, that his family could see him, and that the Government would have to produce him in court.

It did not take long for the Prime Minister to find out that my husband and I had been to see Azizah. On the television news that night, Prime Minister Mahathir was asked about our call on Azizah. What did he think of that? He replied, "It's OK to visit. Just don't tell lies."

We still wonder what that meant. Don't send false reports to the State Department?

The State Department's official position on Anwar's arrest was that it hoped for a fair trial, but it took no position on the question of Anwar's guilt or innocence. It was a neutral position, and that was the same official position that my husband took.

But the fact that we paid a personal and private call on our friend Azizah caused a lot of waves and interest around KL. There was great personal sympathy and concern for Azizah among many other Ambassadors' wives as well, for Azizah had always been kind and friendly to all of us.

And something else happened that was very interesting.

As we would travel through Kuala Lumpur on our way to various events, people would see the American flag flying on the front of the Ambassador's car. And for the first time during our three year stay in Malaysia, Malaysians would honk and wave and smile at us. It was their way of saying "thank you" for our visit to Azizah.

Malaysians would walk up to us at receptions and other events and whisper in our ear, "Thank you for what you did." They whispered to us, for they dared not say it in public.

2

The Day After

Azizah speaks and calms an angry crowd:
"We must not use violence."

THE DAY AFTER

It was the early morning hours of September 21, just hours after the arrest that shook Malaysia. Anwar's house in the Bukit Damansara section of Kuala Lumpur was surrounded by the police and their armored vehicles.

The house was also surrounded by thousands of Anwar's supporters.

The door was unlocked. The police would come and go into the house, as did journalists. Close friends and relatives were there to comfort Azizah and her children.

But there were few others who dared to come. Most of the politicians and businessmen who were close to Anwar—who sought his favor and friendship—now were nowhere to be seen.

Then Azizah appeared before hundreds of supporters. There was tremendous anger among them about what had happened the night before. Even as the police surrounded the house, Azizah summoned the courage to speak openly to her husband's supporters. And she said:

> "We must not use any violence to achieve the objectives of the Reformasi[1] movement. We will proceed only in a peaceful manner."

Azizah spoke in a calm manner. She knew that Malaysia must avoid the violence and chaos that had affected its neighbor Indonesia only a few months before. Malaysia has always feared that this kind of turmoil would turn into a racial confrontation.

Malaysia is a country where people of many races, cultures, and religions live together. And that is what makes Malaysia such a fascinating country. Its population is 22 million. The ethnic Malays, who are Muslims, and other local peoples are about 60%; the ethnic Chinese are 30%; and ethnic Indians are 10%.

---

1. After Anwar was fired by Prime Minister Mahathir in September 1998, he went on a nationwide speaking tour and called for political and economic reform in Malaysia. His movement became known as *"Reformasi,"* which is the Malay word for reform.

Prime Minister Mahathir's policy was based on promoting the progress of the Malays, while ensuring that there is racial harmony between the Chinese and Malays. Anwar followed the same policy.

In general, the Malays dominate Malaysia's political system, while the Chinese are active on the economic stage. They work hard to respect each other's cultures and religions, and to maintain a society that lives in harmony. And in the end, all of them say proudly, "I am a Malaysian!"

Anwar is Malay and a Muslim, but his criticism of corruption and cronyism in the Government and his belief that everyone in Malaysia should be lifted from poverty, no matter what their race, appealed to people throughout the country.

Why should the mantle of political leadership now fall on Azizah? Why should this "housewife" and mother be the one to address the crowds?

After Anwar's arrest, his closest political aides also were arrested.

But there was another reason. As Anwar's wife, it was only natural that people would look to Azizah for guidance and leadership. The person who was closest to Anwar was his wife.

Before Anwar was arrested, he said to his wife, "Azizah, if anything happens to me, you take over."

> "My husband and I have been married for many years and we share the same views and beliefs. So he has faith in me. I must carry the torch that he has passed to me. So I will fight for justice."

But Azizah would need to tread carefully. Mahathir threatened her with arrest not once but twice. He even threatened Azizah's 19-year daughter, saying, "I hope the police do not need to arrest her." But he dared not carry through with his threats. Not only the international reaction, but also the reaction among the Malays would have been overwhelming.

By coincidence, this day, September 21, the day after Anwar was arrested, was when the closing ceremony of the Commonwealth Games[2] was to be held. Malaysia had staked its national pride on these Games, and Queen Elizabeth had just arrived in Kuala Lumpur.

And at the very moment when Azizah was appealing for calm among Anwar's supporters, the arrival ceremony for the Queen and Prince Philip was being held at Parliament Square.

There were the King and Queen of Malaysia, Prime Minister and Mrs. Mahathir, Malaysia's Cabinet Ministers and their wives, and our colleagues, the Ambassadors from over 80 countries around the world and their spouses.

The ceremony came off perfectly. But I couldn't help thinking—at all the other VIP arrival ceremonies my husband and I had attended, Anwar and his wife were present. But they were not here today—suddenly their lives had taken a dramatic turn.

As we waited for the ceremony to start, no one in the diplomatic corps could stop talking about what had happened the night before.

But then Queen Elizabeth and Prince Philip walked over to greet us, followed by Malaysia's King and Queen, and then Prime Minister Mahathir and his wife. We all fell silent. It was such a strange feeling.

That night, the closing ceremony of the Commonwealth Games was held. Prime Minister Mahathir entered the stadium, and there was applause for him. But as Queen Elizabeth spoke, I still kept thinking about Azizah. If it had been the way it should have been, Azizah and her children would have been there too, enjoying the pageantry and the fireworks.

I wondered, why do such things happen?

---

2.   The Commonwealth Games are sort of a "mini-Olympics," held among the countries of the British Commonwealth.

And I still ask that question today. Why is Anwar in jail? He did not kill anyone. He did not steal money. And why have these terrible things happened to such wonderful people as Azizah and her family?

I left the ceremony with some Malaysian friends, but it was not the right atmosphere to talk about Anwar's arrest. These were younger people who had been supportive of Anwar and the hope that he gave them for Malaysia's future. But I couldn't ask them anything, because I knew that they now were fearful for their own future. If they spoke in support of Anwar, they risked being arrested. They risked losing business contracts. They risked being ostracized.

As Anwar said after he was arrested, "If this can happen to me, the Deputy Prime Minister, then it can happen to anyone who opposes Mahathir."

As we drove home, there were police everywhere. And then one of the passengers pointed to a building and said, "I think that is where Anwar is being held by the police."

And what was happening to Anwar at that same moment? We had no idea, but eight days later we would find out—and receive one of the shocks of our lives.

3

Why It Happened

The Anwar that the world knew

WHY IT HAPPENED

Just 20 days before his arrest, Anwar had been fired by Mahathir as Deputy Prime Minister and ousted from his position as Vice President of the United Malay National Organization (UMNO), the leading political party in the Government.

And in the following three weeks, Anwar launched a campaign throughout the country. People came from all over the countryside to hear him speak.

Their numbers increased daily. Thousands, and then tens of thousands came to listen to him. This was the greatest political challenge that Mahathir had ever faced.

Hundreds of people were arrested in Malaysia simply for shouting the word, "Reformasi" (reform).

Azizah joined Anwar, standing by his side at all these speeches.

How did it happen? How did Anwar, the Deputy Prime Minister and heir apparent, end up as an outsider, challenging his former mentor, Mahathir Mohamed?

A few months before Anwar was fired, a small booklet appeared in Kuala Lumpur called "*50 Reasons Why Anwar Cannot Become Prime Minister.*" It was said by many people that this booklet was backed by people close to Prime Minister Mahathir, people who were afraid of what would happen to them if Anwar became Prime Minister.

To preserve their political power and avoid any investigation of their business dealings and corruption, they needed to stop Anwar.

The booklet accused Anwar of abuse of power, corruption, homosexuality, womanizing, treason, murder, being a CIA spy, and on and on. The number of sins and crimes he was accused of were beyond imagination.

In most situations, accusations like this would be dismissed out of hand.

But as ludicrous as the book was, it had a different purpose—to kill Anwar politically. Copies of the book were given to every delegate to UMNO's national political meeting.[1]

Who ordered this? Who paid for all the copies? At that moment, Anwar was UMNO's Deputy Party President, and he had many supporters within the UMNO Party. So who authorized this attack on the party's second-highest leader?

Shortly after the party convention, Prime Minister Mahathir expelled Anwar from the party and also fired him as Deputy Prime Minister. Mahathir said that the reason he fired Anwar was his low morals. Specifically, he said Anwar was a homosexual—a sin in Islam—and that Anwar had used his government position to try and influence a police investigation into his alleged sins.

As for Anwar, he said, "There is no truth to this. This is a conspiracy to destroy me politically."

Azizah believed in her husband and said,

> "They say that my husband is a sex maniac and a homosexual, and that he had a love child. They say that to hide that, he committed murder. They claim that he is a foreign spy and a traitor. The list of sins goes on and on.
>
> "My family must protect its name. I believe in my husband's innocence. And I believe that in the end, justice will prevail."

But to understand how all this came about in 1998, we need to understand what had happened a year before.

In the early summer of 1997, Prime Minister Mahathir decided to do something that he had never done before. He decided to take a vacation for two months, and go to South America and Europe. He wanted to write a book about

---

1.   UMNO, or the United Malay National Organization, has been the dominant and ruling political party in Malaysia since independence in 1957. Its leader as Party President is Prime Minister Mahathir.

his success in developing Malaysia.[2] He would turn the reins of government over to Anwar.

It was a great symbol of trust in his deputy. And it also was a clear indication that one day, when Mahathir decided to retire, Anwar would replace him as Prime Minister of Malaysia.

During his two months as Acting Prime Minister, Anwar sent a number of signals about what life would be like in Malaysia when he became Prime Minister. He launched investigations into corruption. He indicated that he would focus not on building huge shopping centers and skyscrapers in Kuala Lumpur, but on building low-cost housing and improving the welfare of the poorer people in the countryside.

As his time as Acting Prime Minister was coming to an end, Anwar launched a Malaysian Peace Corps, called *Wawasan*. As one of the most successful developing economies in the world, Malaysia has much to teach other developing countries in a very practical way.

I went to the ceremony that started *Wawasan*, and it was remarkable to see how many people—politicians and big businessmen—all wanted to be close to Anwar. There were nearly 2,000 people there—the largest gathering I had attended in KL.

They saw the future, and there was great enthusiasm.

But there were other people who saw the future, and they were frightened.

Some businessmen were afraid that they would lose their political connections and their contracts.

Some political leaders were afraid that they would lose their access to power.

---

2.   I believe that Prime Minister Mahathir deserves great credit for Malaysia's economic development. But at the same time, it is very clear that during his 20 years as Prime Minister, he has become more authoritarian, and the rights of the Malaysian people have been curtailed. We have a saying in Japan: "Even the purest of water can turn stagnant if it stays in the same place too long."

Others were frightened that they could become the target of an investigation into their corruption.

So they decided that they had to stop Anwar. Their political and business survival required them to do whatever they had to do in order to stop Anwar.

So some of them gathered to start a "poison pen letter" campaign against Anwar. Poison pen letters are very common in Malaysia. People hesitate to say certain things in public, so they write a letter instead.

The letter went to Mahathir, but he ignored it. He still supported Anwar.

So why was it, that one year later, when the very same accusations were made against Anwar, this time Mahathir decided to support it and do everything he could to destroy Anwar?

Why was it that the book,"*50 Reasons Why Anwar Cannot Become Prime Minister*," now was placed in the folders of UMNO members?

Why did Mahathir change his mind?

The immediate cause was the Asian financial crisis.

When Mahathir was on vacation in France, the Thai economy collapsed and the so-called contagion spread throughout Asia, including to Malaysia. By the time he came back to Malaysia, Mahathir was very angry. He thought that all of his hard work in developing Malaysia the past 18 years had been destroyed. He was mad at Anwar for listening to the International Monetary Fund (IMF) and others about what to do about the economy.

So Mahathir began speaking out. But every time he spoke, it made the situation worse. The stock market would fall and the ringgit (Malaysia's currency) would get cheaper. Meanwhile, Anwar was doing everything he could to try and stop the damage that Mahathir's rhetoric was causing.

There is no doubt that Anwar and Mahathir had very different views about how to handle the financial crisis.

In the beginning, the Malaysian Government as a whole went along with Anwar. He was supported and advised by the officials in the Finance Minister and the Central Bank.

For several months, the people supported Anwar. And you could see this in subtle ways. At the Islamic New Year[3] in February 1998, Mahathir and Anwar both held Open House receptions at about the same time. They lived near each other. When we left Anwar's home, there were about 200 people there, all having fun. When we arrived at the Prime Minister's Residence across the street, there were fewer people there. People noticed this, and they talked about it.

But Malaysian businessmen were feeling great pain. They had borrowed too much money, and now they could not pay it back. They would complain to Mahathir about what Anwar was doing. They wanted low interest rates and government support. Anwar had cut back government public works contracts, and many of these businessmen were involved in construction.

By the spring of 1998, the Malaysian economy still had not recovered, and more people started to ask when Anwar's policies would start to produce benefits for them.

Mahathir wanted the Government to help rescue certain prominent businessmen, but Anwar refused.

More and more, they were at odds.

Then in Indonesia, the Suharto Government fell, and Anwar's friend Habibie became the President. There were changes of Government in Thailand and Korea as well. New leaders—opposed to corruption and cronyism—were taking charge across Asia, and they were friends of Anwar's.

Now the economic conflict between the two men also became a political conflict. Some of Anwar's supporters started to push him to challenge Mahathir politically. They said that Mahathir's rhetoric was hurting the country's econ-

---

3.   Known throughout the Muslim world as Eid'il Fitri and in Malaysia as Hari Raya, this celebrates the end of Ramadan, the Muslim fasting month.

omy, so he should go. They told Anwar that he should do something. The future of the country was at stake.

Anwar then made a few speeches that said if Malaysia's Government leaders do not listen to the voice of the people and stamp out corruption and cronyism, then they will go the way of Suharto in Indonesia.

Mahathir was listening—and he saw it as a direct challenge to his political leadership. He believed that Anwar wanted to remove him as Prime Minister.

So now the poison pen letters that were hidden in the drawer for one year were pulled out.

The accusations against Anwar that were false one year before, now suddenly became true.

Anwar must be stopped.

Anwar must be destroyed politically.

In the space of a few days, Mahathir fired the Governor of the Central Bank.

Then he appointed one of his closest associates, Tun Daim Zainuddin, as his Financial Advisor, in a direct challenge to Anwar's position as Finance Minister.

He imposed capital controls on money going in and out of Malaysia.

And he fixed the value of the ringgit at 3.8 to the dollar, turning the clock back almost 30 years, when the world did away with fixed exchange rates.

Mahathir believed that now, he had achieved control of his country's economy.

Now, the next step was to ensure that his political control of the country was unchallenged.

Anwar's economic power had been taken away.

And now Anwar's political power must be destroyed.

4

Where is Anwar?

Anwar addresses a crowd of nearly 100,000 people
in Malaysia's Merdeka (Independence) Square,
as Azizah stands by his side.
The next day, he was arrested.

WHERE IS ANWAR?

When the police took Anwar away the night they arrested him, they put Azizah in the same car. But when they were a short distance away, where the crowd and photographers could no longer see them, they stopped the car. The police made Azizah and her family get into a different vehicle, and then they drove away with Anwar.

She had no idea where they took him.

After Anwar's arrest, people came to Azizah with unsettling reports. Anwar has been beaten. He is in the hospital. No—he is dead.

Azizah was so concerned about Anwar's safety that in an interview with CNBC she repeated a report that she had heard. She expressed her fear that to prove that Anwar was a homosexual, the police would inject him with the AIDS virus.

The police were angry at what she said and called her to police headquarters. They warned her, "If you make these kinds of statements, we will arrest you, too, under the Internal Security Act."

After that, Azizah's ability to speak out was curtailed. She had lost her freedom of speech. If she said anything that the police did not like, they would arrest her.

She was now in a position where it was hard for her to defend her husband against all these accusations, and it also was hard to continue his political reform movement. She would have to choose her words carefully.

And the police told her that she was prohibited from speaking at rallies of Anwar's supporters.

> "I kept wondering what would happen to the children if I were arrested under the ISA like my husband. My little one, Hana, asked my eldest daughter, "Izzah, if Mommy is arrested, will you take care of me?"

I will never forget the look in Azizah's eyes when she told me that story.

The orders went down to prohibit rallies by Anwar supporters anywhere in the country. Political gatherings in mosques also were forbidden.

On September 24, 5000 people defied that order. They gathered peacefully after prayers at a mosque.

When they left the mosque, the police opened fire on them with tear gas and water cannon. The water was colored with a special yellow dye that stained clothing. So even if the demonstrators ran away, the police would chase them into stores and shopping centers and arrest them.

But overall, Kuala Lumpur was generally peaceful, and there was no need to fear for one's safety. Most people were able to carry on with their daily lives. Schools and businesses were open, as were the restaurants and stores. Visitors from abroad were surprised to see that the streets were peaceful. There was nothing like the violence and chaos that had taken place in Jakarta.

But Prime Minister Mahathir said at a press conference, "Until Anwar tells his supporters to stop their violence, he will remain in jail."

Anwar, of course, was in jail, being held under the ISA. No one knew where he was, and he was not allowed to see anyone. So one journalist asked the Prime Minister the very logical question, "How can Anwar do that, when he is in jail?" Mahathir replied, "I don't know. Maybe mental telepathy?"

The Government's criticism of Anwar continued, but in the midst of that, there were more and more voices expressing concern about Anwar. For Anwar had not been seen since his arrest. The rumors did not stop.

Anwar's lawyers told the press that they were not allowed to meet their client, and in fact they even did not know where he was.

For all practical purposes, Anwar had disappeared! Where is Anwar? Is he safe?

Day by day, the voice of the people grew stronger. The Government must produce Anwar!

The police authorities could no longer ignore those pleas. So at a press conference, the Inspector General of Police[1], Abdul Rahim Noor, said, "Anwar is safe and sound."

But the truth was different. Rahim had lied to the world.

At that moment, Anwar was in a life and death situation.

Not only that. In fact, it was Rahim, the IGP, the man who said, "Anwar is safe and sound," who had beaten Anwar nearly to death with his own fists. And even on that very day, when Rahim lied to the world at his press conference, Anwar was still in his jail cell, being denied medical attention.

It would not be until March 1999, six months later, that the truth would be revealed.

---

1.   Malaysia has a national police force, and the Inspector General of Police, or IGP, is the nation's top law enforcement officer and the commander of the nation's entire police force.

5

The World Gets a Shock: Anwar's Black Eye

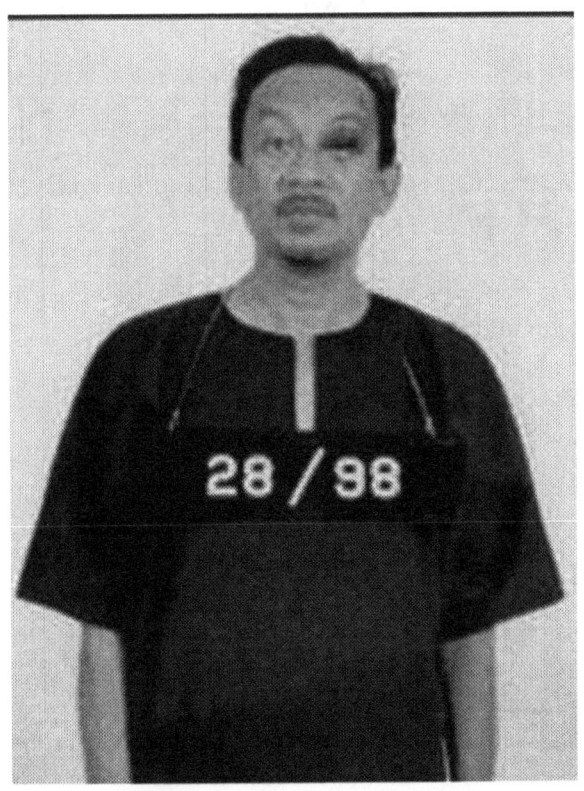

Prisoner 28/98, with the infamous black eye

THE WORLD GETS A SHOCK: ANWAR'S BLACK EYE

On September 29, 1998, nine days after he was arrested, Anwar finally was brought before the public for the first time, when he was produced in court.

And when the former Deputy Prime Minister of Malaysia appeared in court, the shock reverberated around the entire world. That day will forever be part of Malaysia's history.

What did the world see when Anwar entered the courtroom?

A black circle around Anwar's left eye. A neck brace. Noticeable weight loss. Cuts and bruises. Difficulty in walking.

Once in court, the charges were read out: corruption and sexual misconduct. Anwar rejected them all. "I plead not guilty."

Because Anwar was still being held under the ISA, his lawyers were not allowed to speak on his behalf.

Anwar then said to the judge that he had been beaten by the police:

> "On the night of my arrest, I was blindfolded and handcuffed from behind, from the moment that I was separated from my family. In the cell I was also kept blindfolded and handcuffed with my hands behind my back, when I heard footsteps approach me. I stood up as a sign of respect, and without warning I felt a rain of blows. The most painful was into my left eye, which felt like a karate chop over the left side of my neck....And as I started to stand up, I was punched on both sides of my face and neck. I started to bleed from my nose, I lost my vision, and I was beaten until I was unconscious. Even now, I cannot see well from my left eye. And if I am not supported, I have a hard time to walk."

Azizah was in court, learning and seeing for the first time what had happened to her husband. With her were her 19-year old daughter Izzah and her 16-year old daughter Nuha, as well as Anwar's parents.

Azizah is a medical doctor—an ophthalmologist, no less—and she gave an on-the-spot eye exam to her husband.

She then told the judge:

> "My husband has an orbital hematoma in his left eye and a small depression on his left forehead. His vision is impaired."

And to the press after the hearing, she said she was stunned by what she had seen:

> "I can't believe they went this far…"

The picture of Anwar with the black eye was front page news around the world.

The U.S. Department of State, the Prime Minister of Australia, and others called for an investigation into Anwar's beating and repeated their hopes for a fair trial. The Foreign Secretary of the United Kingdom, UN Secretary General Kofi Annan, Amnesty International, and many others issued statements asking that Anwar's rights be protected.

But from the Japanese Government, there was nothing. According to the AFP press service, when they asked the Japanese Foreign Ministry for a comment, they replied, "Our stance, which remains the same as before, is that making any comments on their internal affairs would be inappropriate."

In Malaysia the voices calling for a fair trial for Anwar only increased.

But the newspapers and television stations of Malaysia, which are controlled by the government, never reported those voices. Out on the streets, however, there was anger about Anwar's black eye, and a belief that the police had gone too far. On the internet, websites supporting Anwar sprouted up all over.

With anger about Anwar's black eye growing across the country, Prime Minister Mahathir held a press conference and made a shocking statement.

He said that it was "not impossible" that Anwar might have beaten himself up, "as he will gain much mileage if it can be shown that he is being tortured by the police."

When Azizah heard this, she said, "I am shocked that someone who is a medical doctor[1] would make such a comment without examining the patient."

Prime Minister Mahathir's comment that Anwar might have beaten himself up was reported around the world. Seeing what had happened to Anwar and how Mahathir reacted to it, voices of criticism started to rise from the leaders of other Asian countries, who had been silent until then. President Estrada of the Philippines said that because his friend Anwar had been beaten up, he might decide not to attend the Asia Pacific Economic Cooperation (APEC) meetings[2] that would be held in Kuala Lumpur in November 1998. President Habibie of Indonesia said, "I am really worried about my friend Anwar, and I might cancel my participation in APEC."

Now it appeared the Anwar incident would have an effect on November's APEC meetings.

Months went by, but public dissatisfaction only increased. After a police investigation curiously failed to find out who was responsible for beating Anwar, Prime Minister Mahathir agreed to establish a Royal Commission of Inquiry to investigate the Black Eye Incident.

And as a result of that inquiry, it became absolutely clear that it was Rahim Noor, the Inspector General of Police, who had beaten Anwar. The Commission also reported that in fact the beating was so severe that it was a "life-threatening situation," and that Anwar had been left without medical attention for four days.

Indeed, the Government doctor who examined Anwar after the beating testified, "He is lucky that he is still alive."

In March 1999 Rahim pleaded guilty and was sentenced to six months imprisonment. Later, on appeal, it was reduced to two months. But even as this is written (July 2000) the man who abused his powers as Inspector General of Police—the man who almost killed the former Deputy Prime Minister of Malay-

---

1.   Prime Minister Mahathir practiced medicine before he entered politics.
2.   APEC, or Asia Pacific Economic Cooperation, is a gathering of the leaders of 21 economies in the Asia Pacific region, including China, Japan, Korea, the United States, Canada, Australia, Russia, Mexico, India and others.

sia and who presided over a cover-up of his actions—has not yet served even one day in jail.[3]

Meanwhile, the man who was accused only of interfering in a police investigation, Anwar Ibrahim, ended up being sentenced to six years in prison.

---

3.   At the time of printing of this English edition, Rahim in fact has served his jail time, although he was released after 40 days.

6

Azizah Meets Secretary of State Madeline Albright

A cordial and very personal meeting

AZIZAH MEETS
SECRETARY OF STATE
MADELINE ALBRIGHT

Ten days after Anwar appeared in court with his back eye, the Government amended the charges. No longer was Anwar held under the ISA. Now he was accused of corruption[1] and sexual deviancy under the criminal code.

The trial began on November 2, 1998.

For Azizah, who had been filled with anxiety for so long, the start of the trial was a kind of step forward. Now, together with her family, she could see Anwar in court, and talk to him, and confirm with her own eyes his physical condition. Even if he was on trial, it was a far better situation than when he had "disappeared" under the ISA and been beaten by the head of Malaysia's national police.

> "I am worried about his physical condition, but his spirit is high," she said.

And in turn, Anwar also offered encouragement to Azizah and his family, to be strong.

Anwar's defense team was filled with top lawyers, all serving as volunteers without pay. Sitting in the courtroom were representatives of international human rights groups and foreign embassies who came to monitor the fairness of the trial.

As soon as the court proceedings began, the government's key witness, a senior police inspector, testified, "If I am ordered by my superiors to lie, then I will do so."

It was a startling statement. How could anyone be sure of the truthfulness of what he now was going to say? But the judge, Augustine Paul, said nothing, and the trial continued.

---

1. This is not corruption in a financial or monetary sense. In American law, the comparable charge would be "obstruction of justice" or "abuse of power."

Throughout the trial, the many websites about Anwar that had started on the internet allowed the Malaysian people to read the news that their own papers would not publish.

After the black eye incident, Azizah received messages of encouragement from Anwar's friends around the world. And everyday Anwar's supporters stood outside the courthouse, offering support and cheers for Azizah and her family whenever they appeared.

Azizah started traveling into the countryside to make speeches. Thousands of people would come to see her, even in the midst of tropical downpours.

Her eldest daughter Izzah made a surprise visit to the Philippines to see President Estrada and to Indonesia to see President Habibie. They were both her father's friends, and she appealed for their support.

Meanwhile, the APEC meetings would soon be held in Kuala Lumpur. Reporters came from around the world to cover the meetings, which would attract the leaders of the United States, Japan and China, and many other countries in the Pacific region.

Many of those reporters also wanted to interview Azizah, the woman who was calling for democracy, justice, and reform in her country. Suddenly Azizah was in the world spotlight, a place she never expected to be. In those interviews, Azizah said very clearly, "My role is to be a symbol of Reformasi."

The APEC meetings in 1998 took place in the midst of Asia's financial crisis, and the situation was even more confused because of the political turmoil in the host country, Malaysia.

There were many reports saying that President Estrada and President Habibie might not attend the meetings, as a protest against what had happened to their friend Anwar Ibrahim. In the end they both came, but it put both of them in a difficult situation.

At the same time, there were voices in the United States Congress saying that the APEC meetings should be moved to another country, something that clearly was impossible to do at that late date.

There were others saying that President Clinton should boycott the APEC Leaders Meeting that would be hosted by Prime Minister Mahathir. After all, they said, Prime Minister Mahathir boycotted the meeting hosted by President Clinton in Seattle in 1993.

But the State Department reminded everyone of the importance of APEC, an organization that the United States supported. So the White House announced that while President Clinton would attend the APEC meetings as planned, he would not have a bilateral meeting with Prime Minister Mahathir.

In Kuala Lumpur, the U.S. Embassy was extremely busy preparing for the APEC meetings. In fact, the preparations had started one year before. As APEC drew nearer, staff employees came to help from the State Department, the White House, and other U.S. Embassies all over Asia.

The APEC meetings would be attended not just by the President, but also the Secretaries of State, Commerce, Treasury, and Agriculture; the U.S. Trade Representative; the National Security Advisor; and senior officials from the White House and other Government departments.

And then there was the press corps that follows the President everywhere—usually about 400 people.

By the time the meetings began, the U.S. Embassy in Kuala Lumpur had issued over 1,200 credentials to these official visitors.

President Clinton planned to greet the Embassy staff at our Official Residence, so White House staff members and Secret Service agents came in and out of our house everyday. They sent two limousines for the President and even a Marine helicopter.

It seemed like the entire White House was coming to Malaysia with the President.

But as we were getting ready for the President to come, there was some bad news.

Tensions were increasing with Iraq. Saddam Hussein had refused to accept a United Nations nuclear weapons inspection team. Depending on how things developed, there was a possibility that there would be air strikes on Iraq. If that happened, then Clinton would have no choice but to cancel his trip to APEC.

At the same time, rumors were circulating in KL that Clinton would meet with Azizah during his visit to Malaysia. My husband told Washington that since the White House had announced that Clinton would not meet with Mahathir, it would be seen as a great insult in Malaysia if Clinton met with Azizah instead. The Embassy put out a press release saying that while Clinton's schedule did not permit a meeting, Secretary of State Albright looked forward to a meeting, if it could be arranged.

On the possibility of an Albright-Azizah meeting, Prime Minister Mahathir said, "This is interference in our internal affairs." By saying this, he hoped that he could put some pressure on other foreign leaders coming to APEC not to meet with Azizah.

But Secretary Albright wanted to meet with Azizah. Albright was a great supporter of another Asian woman who was struggling for freedom and justice, Aung Sang Suu Kyi of Burma, the Nobel Peace Prize winner, and she saw Azizah in the same light.

With Secretary Albright's desires clear, my husband started planning for a meeting. The conclusion was that it would take place in a private setting at our Residence. The visitors from Washington were surprised when my husband said that I would be the one to get in touch with Azizah. He simply said, "They are friends."

But even though we said this was a private meeting, we all knew that it would be filled with great significance.

It was November 14, 1998.

Secretary Albright arrived in Malaysia, even as tensions with Iraq continued to build. Because of that, she had to cut her three day visit back to just one day, canceling almost all of her program in Malaysia. But she still hoped for a visit with Azizah.

So I suddenly had to get in touch with Azizah to change all the plans—the date, the time, the location. I was concerned that Azizah's home telephone was being monitored by the police, and her cellphone as well. So I just went directly to her house.

The meeting between Albright and Azizah now would take place at the hotel where Albright and the U.S. delegation to APEC were staying. For security reasons, the hotel was surrounded by Malaysian police, and there were press people everywhere.

Now we were concerned that because the time and place of the meeting had been announced, something might happen before Azizah got to the hotel. The police might try to stop her vehicle in order to prevent the meeting. So how would we get Azizah and her daughter Izzah to the hotel?

After changing vehicles here and there, in the end Azizah and her daughter rode to the hotel in an Embassy car, just behind my husband and myself, because the police would not stop a diplomatic vehicle heading to the U.S. delegation's hotel.

Our two Embassy vehicles arrived at the hotel without incident. When they saw Azizah get out of one of them, a Special Branch[2] officer angrily asked the Embassy drivers, "How did you get here?" The police were angry that despite their efforts, they could not stop Azizah from meeting with Madeline Albright. They did not know what had happened.

Meanwhile, my husband was happy that the plan succeeded. He said he felt like James Bond.

As soon as Azizah got out of the car, there was an incredible rush of reporters and cameramen coming towards her, perhaps 50 people. There were microphones pointed at her and flash bulbs going off everywhere. They were shouting, "There she is! There she is!" as they came running at her.

---

2. Special Branch, or the SB, is a division of the national police that functions much like the FBI in the United States. It conducts criminal investigations, counter-terrorism, and counter-narcotic work. However, it also engages in domestic political surveillance on behalf of the Government.

It was a chaotic scene. While she had been giving interviews to individual reporters, I don't think that Azizah had ever encountered the aggressive Western press corps all together in a mob before. Each one of them was trying to get a comment and pushing their microphones in her face. I was walking slightly behind Azizah when she grabbed my hand and pulled me up close to her and said, "Hiroko, you stay with me."

I often think about those words and what they mean. For even today, even though we are an ocean part, I still try to stay with Azizah.

The State Department Diplomatic Security agents came to "rescue" us from the press and led us to the elevators. Azizah continued to hold my hand.

Of course I could not join my husband and Secretary Albright in the meeting. But I saw Azizah when she came out, and she looked so happy. I had the impression that Secretary Albright really shared her strength with Azizah and gave her encouragement.

When we went back to the lobby, the press was more orderly. The Embassy's press officers had put them behind a rope! Their numbers had increased to well over a hundred. My husband was escorting Azizah and Izzah through the lobby, and I was walking behind. But once again, Azizah reached around and grabbed me!

The press was shouting questions at her, so she stopped for a moment at the press rope. She replied with confidence, and with that same gentle voice.

> *"How did the meeting go?"*
>
> "I'm very happy with the meeting."
>
> *"What did you talk about with Secretary Albright?"*
>
> "We had a lot of support from Secretary Albright."
>
> *"What kind of support?"*
>
> "It's moral support."

The meeting ended without incident, and we returned to the Residence about 8:30 at night. Azizah seemed very happy and relaxed. And then she said,

"Hiroko, I haven't eaten since this afternoon. Could I bother you? I'm really hungry!"

We all laughed. It was a Sunday, and I had dismissed the Residence staff earlier that day. So I opened up the refrigerator to see what was there. As we dined on warmed-up *satay* and homemade chocolate chip cookies, we relived the evening.

My husband told Azizah that over the years he had been in dozens and dozens of meetings with the Secretaries of State, and that he could not think of any visitor who had handled herself more brilliantly in a meeting than Azizah. "It was very impressive," he said. "A-Plus."

During APEC, Azizah was invited to a luncheon with the Canadian Foreign and Trade Ministers, and she also met the Foreign Minister of Australia. Finally, she called on the man who proudly said he was a friend of Anwar, President Estrada of the Philippines.

Azizah now was getting moral support from all directions, from the leaders of both Asian and Western nations.

Among all these meetings, perhaps the one with the greatest personal significance was with Secretary Albright, another woman who has dealt with adversity. Albright's relatives were persecuted and even killed because of their Jewish religion. Albright herself was a refugee twice, first from the Nazis and then from the Communists. She came to America, and she had risen to the top of the U.S. Government. As a divorced mother, she earned a PhD while raising her children.

Like Azizah, Madeline Albright was a woman who suddenly found herself face-to-face with great challenges, and she overcame then. I think that more than the political significance of meeting with the U.S. Secretary of State, the personal significance of meeting such a woman offered encouragement to Azizah.

After the meeting, the State Department's spokesman, Nicholas Burns, said, "The symbolic gesture of meeting with Azizah, saying that we remember and care about the case, is very important."

In effect, Albright's message to Azizah and to the people and Government of Malaysia was that we will not forget what has happened to Anwar, and that we have a great interest in what is going to happen there in the future.

We will not forget his arrest under the ISA and the violations of his human rights. We will not forget his beating by the head of the police. We will not forget the threats to Azizah and her family.

And it is not just the United States. It is the whole world that is saying, "We will not forget."

7

Vice President Gore's Speech Backfires

The day after his controversial speech, Gore wore
a colorful Malaysian batik shirt
as he shook hands with Prime Minister Mahathir

VICE PRESIDENT GORE'S SPEECH BACKFIRES

The day after Azizah met Madeline Albright, we heard that Clinton cancelled his trip to APEC at the last moment because of the Iraq situation. Vice President Gore would represent him. Gore boarded Air Force One, which already was fueled and waiting to fly to KL.

When the Embassy staff and visitors heard this, they were disappointed, and so were the staff from the White House and the Secret Service. It was a real let-down for them. They had worked so hard to get ready for the President, and now the Number Two was coming.

The Malaysians I knew also were very disappointed that Clinton was not coming.

Almost all of the 400 reporters who were planning to come with Clinton canceled their visit. Only ten or so came with Gore.

I realized what a difference it makes whether you are the President or the Vice President!

Vice President Gore arrived on November 16, 1998.

That night the business leaders from the APEC economies had organized an APEC Business Summit dinner. Prime Minister Mahathir would be there, along with the other APEC leaders. In the audience would be over 1,000 business leaders from throughout the Asia-Pacific region.

From the beginning, it was planned that President Clinton would be the guest speaker. The organizers really wanted Clinton because they knew he would draw a lot of attention.

But now Clinton could not come, and Gore was the substitute. But even though Gore was not the President, the organizers decided that he should be the substitute speaker. So the American Vice President was given the nod in preference to the Presidents and Prime Ministers of other countries. He would read Clinton's speech at the APEC dinner.

Any Presidential speech overseas is based on ideas and information that the State Department and the Embassy provide, but in the end it is written in the White House. The State Department provides a draft speech. Then it goes to the National Security Council and then to the President's speechwriters, who make changes. And in the end, it goes to the President, who makes his own changes and approves it.

Vice President Gore delivered the speech that President Clinton was supposed to make, although in the end he made the final decisions about what he would say.

My husband never saw the final text of the speech until two hours before the dinner started. And when he read it, he saw one sentence that he knew was going to cause a real problem.

Even if America wanted to express support for the goals of democracy and freedom that the Reformasi movement was fighting for, my husband thought that this was not the place or the way to do it. As Ambassador, he told Vice President Gore that if he read that sentence, it would hurt the reform movement. The Mahathir Government would claim that the Reformasi movement was being supported by America, and there would be a negative reaction from most Malaysians.

Even as we sat in the car going to the dinner site, my husband was on the car phone, talking to the Vice President's staff. They promised to report his concerns to the Vice President again.

In the hall were 1,000 smiling, happy faces of business leaders and government officials from throughout the Asia-Pacific region. Then Prime Minister Mahathir and the other leaders entered the hall: President Jiang Xemin of China, President Estrada of the Philippines, President Habibie of Indonesia, Prime Minister Hashimoto of Japan, and others. It was like a "Who's Who" of Asia.

Then Vice President Gore, as the guest speaker, appeared, surrounded by Secret Service agents. Gore shook hands with Prime Minister Mahathir and the other leaders, and then went to the stage to make his speech.

The theme of his speech was the Asian Financial Crisis.

As he spoke, he came closer to the sentence that my husband said should be deleted. Would Gore say it?

And then he read it:

> "Among nations suffering from economic crises, we continue to hear calls for democracy, calls for reform in many languages—People's Power, Doi Moi, Reformasi.[1] We hear them today right here, right now, among the brave people of Malaysia."

The room suddenly was silent, and no one could listen to the rest of the speech. The atmosphere in the room changed dramatically. When the speech was over, there was little applause. His speech finished, Gore shook hands with the other leaders. He and Prime Minister Mahathir had a very cool handshake, and then Gore left the room.

The atmosphere in the room changed immediately. There was a great chill in the air. My husband said, "The temperature is this room has just gone down by 20 degrees." Some people finished their dinner quickly, in silence, and left.

The winds of criticism started to flow throughout the room. Gore's speech is inciting violence! It is interference in Malaysia's internal affairs! It showed no sensitivity—you are invited as a guest, and then you criticize your host to his face! It is an insult to the Malaysian people! You come to dinner, say what you want to, and then you walk out!

It wasn't just the Malaysians. Americans also came up to my husband to complain. And some of them blamed him for what Gore said. They didn't know that my husband had tried to stop it until the last moment.

One businessperson from New York complained, "Because of what Gore did, now I have lost all my Malaysian friends."

---

1.   People's Power referred to the movement that overthrew Marcos in the Philippines; Doi Moi was an economic reform program of the Vietnamese Government; and reformasi was the name of Anwar's reform movement.

Why did Gore leave the dinner early? Actually, the dinner organizers had agreed to this a long time before. When they asked Clinton to speak, the White House staff said that he would not be able to stay through dinner. He would speak, and then leave. The Malaysian organizers said that was all right. And when Gore substituted for Clinton, that still was the plan.

But the organizers failed to tell the audience that Gore would leave after the speech, without staying for dinner. So when he left, whether you were an Asian or an American, it appeared to be a terrible breach of etiquette.

The next morning, the papers in Malaysia were united in condemning what Gore had done.

And the supporters of Reformasi were afraid that Gore's embrace had become the kiss of death.

It was just as my husband predicted. But he told his staff, no matter what we think about this, we must remain loyal to the Vice President. He tried to calm things down and told the Malaysian press that it should focus on Vice President Gore's basic message, which was the importance of democracy.

Those who supported Mahathir were angry, as we knew they would be. And those who supported Anwar were concerned, as we also knew they would be.

Gore's speech had given ammunition to Prime Minister Mahathir's supporters. Now they could say that the Reformasi movement was being supported by foreigners, and that any Malaysian who supported Reformasi was a traitor and a tool of the Americans.

One Reformasi leader quickly issued a press release criticizing Gore.

The Reformasi movement had grown like a spark among the Malaysian masses, but now Gore's speech had poured cold water on that spark.

8

Judgment Day

Trying to keep a cheerful face,
Azizah arrives at court
with daughter Izzah

JUDGMENT DAY

After the APEC meetings were over, Anwar's trial resumed.

Things had not been going well for the prosecution. Their DNA expert had been discredited by expert testimony, making it difficult to prove the sexual allegations against Anwar. So the Government amended the charges halfway through the trial. Now they simply would try to convict Anwar of corruption—that he had interfered in a police investigation. Yet this was an investigation that he had asked the police to conduct.

Azizah and Izzah went to court almost every day. She did not want to think about what the outcome would be. There were so many hurdles that she would have to overcome to prove her husband's innocence and achieve justice.

Just three months before, Azizah, the symbol of Reformasi, had been given the torch of leadership by her husband, Anwar. And the torch was getting heavier and heavier to bear.

Azizah told me how she felt:

> "I never thought even in my dreams that I would ever be in a position like this. Right now I feel like I am in the eye of a hurricane. But the eye of the hurricane is calm, so I must remain calm.

> "As a Muslim, I believe that there is a purpose to everything that happens to us. And in the end, justice will prevail."

Azizah had to balance so many things. To be the mother to six young children who had lost their father and who had a hard time understanding what was happening. To be the wife of her husband, and to attend his trial everyday and give him all the support she could. To be the symbol of Reformasi and to carry on the struggle in the absence of her husband.

And now people around her wanted to add one more duty. They wanted to formally create a new political party and make her its leader.

On April 4, 1999 the Keadilan (Justice) Party was formed, with Anwar's supporters as its base. Wan Azizah became the party's leader, and it had about 100,000 members. The party's slogan was "Reform and Justice."

Its symbol was an eye—although it was light blue, it was to remind people of Anwar's famous black eye.

Although most of its members were Malay, its membership came from all of Malaysia's races. In Malaysia, most political parties are based on race. Prime Minister Mahathir's United Malay National Organization (UMNO) is centered on the Malays, as is the opposition Islamic Party, PAS. The Chinese are in the Malaysian Chinese Association (MCA) or the Democratic Action Party (DAP), and the Indians in the Malaysian Indian Congress (MIC). Because these parties are based on race, they are able to tap into a ready-made pool of voters.

But Keadilan went beyond race. It was a party supported by people who came together because they wanted to reform Malaysia's political system. It is based not on race but on a common political philosophy.

Ten days after Keadilan's founding came the day of judgment in Anwar's first trial.

Azizah led her six children into the courtroom. The children believed that when the trial was over, their Papa would return home. Legal experts who had been monitoring the trial thought that even in the worst-case situation, Anwar would be sentenced to a term of two years or so, based on previous judgments in similar cases.

Then, as Azizah and her children listened, the judge rendered his decision. Anwar was guilty and would be sentenced to six years in prison. Furthermore, he would not be given any credit for the six months he already had spent in jail during the trial.

When she heard Judge Augustine Paul's decision, Anwar's eldest daughter Izzah began to weep. Hana, the youngest daughter, saw the tears falling down her sister's cheeks and asked, "Isn't Papa going to come home?"

One foreign journalist who was covering the trial, Brian Miller, wrote afterwards about Anwar's only son, Ihsan:

> "For the first time in public, Ihsan showed his emotions…and openly wept in court…Anwar walked toward his son and held him in a heartbreaking bear hug…The father whispered something to the son and I heard young Ihsan say, Okay. I will. Okay."

> "Later, when I asked him what his father had told him, he replied, "Papa asked me to be strong. He said I must continue to believe. I must carry on.

> "I can. But I am going to miss Papa."

Anwar's supporters were waiting outside the courthouse for Azizah to appear. She joined her two eldest daughters, Izzah and Nuha, and went to see the crowd. Her son Ihsan and the youngest girls went out a side door and returned home—without their father.

9

Azizah Moves Forward

Azizah celebrates the launch
of her new political party, Keadilan (Justice)

AZIZAH MOVES FORWARD

Four months before Anwar's verdict was handed down, my husband left his post as Ambassador to Malaysia and resigned from the State Department. We came home to America.

But even though we were far away, I could not stop thinking about Azizah and remembering when I went to say farewell to her.

We were shocked by the decision against Anwar and frustrated that there was nothing we could do about it. All we could do was call Azizah to share our feelings.

She said to us:

> "My husband told me, "Don't cry. Be strong. Don't be sad. It is all part of the struggle."

Azizah knew that she would have to be strong—for her husband, for her children, and for her country.

What should we think about Anwar's sentence? It was six years, and that was in addition to the six months that he had already served. And what was his crime? Interfering in a police investigation.

Compared to that, the man who almost killed Anwar, the Inspector General of Police, Abdul Rahim Noor, was only sentenced to six months. Later that sentence was reduced to two months because of Rahim's service to his nation.[1]

But Anwar also served his nation....

Am I the only one who believes that this was a political verdict? When I think of Anwar in jail, I remember Nelson Mandela, who spent 27 years as a political prisoner in South Africa.

Reuters reported my husband's comment on the verdict around the world. He said, "The world needs to understand that Anwar Ibrahim is its newest and most

---

1.   In the end, Rahim, who beat Anwar nearly to death, served only 40 days in jail.

prominent political prisoner." After my husband said that, Amnesty International called Anwar a prisoner of conscience, and one year later the State Department declared Anwar a political prisoner.

Anwar's lawyers appealed his sentence, but it was rejected by the Court of Appeals.

Anwar soon would face a second trial that would accuse him of sodomy. And Azizah would find herself going to court once again.

But now she also was the leader of the Keadilan Party, and elections were coming up, perhaps soon. Her burdens were growing.

The decision on the timing of the elections was up to Prime Minister Mahathir.

Then he decided. The elections would be held on November 29, 1999. That would be only two months after the founding of Keadilan. Azizah threw herself into the preparations for her new party's first elections.

And then something happened for the first time in Malaysia' political history. The opposition parties came together in an alliance called the Barisan Alternatif (BA), or Alternative Front. They agreed to campaign together, and to cooperate on choosing candidates so they would not take votes away from each other.

Azizah decided to run for election from Anwar's Parliamentary district in the northern State of Penang. UMNO, under the leadership of Prime Minister Mahathir, decided to challenge her with one of Anwar's former political secretaries. UMNO worked overtime to defeat Azizah.

For the first time in 18 years, it seemed like there was a genuine political contest in Malaysia.

But the truth is, the opposition parties face numerous obstacles in Malaysia's elections. For example, they are not allowed to sell or distribute their party newspapers except to their own party members. So ordinary people are not able to read what the opposition has to say because the national daily newspapers are all under the influence of the parties that form the Government. The same is true of the three major television networks. Their news directors are all subject to political guidance.

After Anwar was arrested, any editors close to him, whether in the newspapers or in television, were removed.

The newspapers and television in Malaysia really are a public relations or propaganda machine for the Government. When you live in Malaysia, you feel like you meet Prime Minister Mahathir everyday, 365 days, all year long. There is hardly a day when you do not see the Mahathir's picture in the newspapers or on television.

The television news programs almost always begin, "Today, Prime Minister Mahathir....." The opposition parties have no access to television, and their activities and views are not reported. By contrast, in Japan, the public network NHK provides coverage to all candidates, and in America there are political debates.

But when Azizah's Keadilan Party and the opposition asked for access to television during the election campaign, they were told by a Government Minister, "If you want to be on television, start your own broadcast network!"

All Malaysians know that they do not have the freedom to speak and write whatever they would like, or to criticize the current Government. So they are very careful about what they write. In Malaysia, they call this "self-censorship."

The Malaysian people also know that they are not hearing the whole truth in their newspapers and television. That is why they turn to the internet and to foreign news—and to rumors.

And that is why Prime Minister Mahathir always denounces the foreign press and the websites that call for reform and democracy—because he cannot control them.

There was another problem. Over 700,000 new voters registered during the months after Anwar was arrested in September 1998. Almost one year had gone by since they registered, but the election authorities said that they did have time to process their registrations. So they could not vote in the November 1999 elections. Most people believe that many of those new voters would have supported Anwar and Keadilan.

Finally, in order to hold a political meeting or rally, the opposition parties must get permission from the police.

So the odds were against anyone or any party that tries to challenge the Government.

Azizah is a noble woman. But during the campaign, there was rumor-mongering to try and damage her image. People spread false rumors that Azizah and Anwar were going to get a divorce. One of Mahathir's Cabinet Ministers tried to stir up racial tensions and turn Malay voters against Azizah by saying that she was "a daughter of the dragon," meaning that she had Chinese blood.

But through all these personal attacks, Azizah maintained her dignity. Many women who had never shown much interest in politics before, now came to hear her speak. These women were wives and mothers and daughters, too, and they understood and supported Azizah and her family. They believe that the cruel and vengeful treatment that Mahathir gave to them was un-Malay.

Even though UMNO did everything to try and defeat her, Azizah won by a huge margin in her district. Nationally, her new Keadilan party won five seats. While this was not a large number, her new party achieved 11.5% of the national vote, just two months after her party was formed.

The ruling party UMNO lost 22 seats, and for the first time it failed to win even half the seats in Parliament. Some of Mahathir's Cabinet Ministers lost their seats.

But because the Government's coalition included 14 other parties, altogether they won more than two-thirds of the seats. Many political experts think that Mahathir's party did not get even half of the Malay votes, and that it won its seats thanks to Chinese voters, who did not want to vote for the opposition Malay parties out of fear that they were "too Islamic."

So Mahathir's long political rule—already over 18 years—would continue into the future.

As for Azizah, she said:

> "My being chosen as a Member of Parliament—the fact that my party was able to get this many seats and votes—has great significance"

Prime Minister Mahathir was asked what he thought of Azizah's victory.

He replied, "You can get sympathy votes when you go from house to house crying with your daughter. But the question is whether she can contribute anything at all."

But the truth is, Azizah never once cried in public. But the person who has cried in public to gain sympathy is Prime Minister Mahathir. When I lived in Malaysia, I saw him do this twice on the television news.

Some people saw Mahathir's comments about Azizah and the "sympathy vote" as an insult to all Malaysian women. For many people believed that she had handled herself with grace and dignity throughout the past year, an incredibly difficult year, even when she was threatened by the police with arrest. They supported her as well because they believed that what had happened to her husband was wrong. And they also voted for her party because they believed in its principles—democracy, justice, and human rights.

People voted for Azizah not out of sympathy, but because they saw her as a symbol of justice and democracy, because they admired her, and because they believed they she could make an important contribution to Malaysia.

No matter what had happened, Azizah carried herself with dignity. She was a symbol not only of reform. She was a symbol of an indomitable spirit.

Where did Azizah's strength come from? She told the *Los Angeles Times* in an interview:

> "I am a very spiritual person. I read the Koran, and in one of the lines, in Chapter 37, it says God does not give you a burden greater than what you can bear.

> "I am sure that there is wisdom in everything that happens. You can't tell.

"Maybe our ordeal has served to awaken the Malaysian people to the injustice in our society."

10

Anwar On Trial—Again

Each time Anwar arrived at court,
he would wave to the crowd
to encourage them

ANWAR ON TRIAL—AGAIN

After the election, Anwar's second trial resumed. The prosecution charged him and his stepbrother Sukma with sodomy.

Islam forbids sodomy, and it is one of the worst sins that a Muslim can commit. If a person is found guilty of sodomy, it would end their life in both politics and society. Not only Anwar but also his family therefore had to defend their honor and family name against the Government's charges.

How difficult it must be for a wife to sit through such a trial and listen to the testimony, and also for the family.

But the prosecution's case had many problems with the evidence. Perhaps in Japan and most of the countries of Europe and the United States, the case could not even be brought to trial because of the lack of evidence.

Anwar had alibis for where he was on the nights in question. In fact, the condominium where the Government said the crime took place was not even built at the time!

When Anwar's lawyers pointed that out, the case was not dismissed. The prosecutors simply changed it to another date one year later, and the judge accepted what they did!

For those of us who live in democracies, where the rights of citizens are protected from the government, it is hard to believe that such a thing could happen.

The case against Anwar was based on the testimony of just one person. But in Islamic law, there must be four witnesses for such a crime. So even though the Government hoped that Anwar would be discredited among other Muslims, it was never able to discredit him in the eyes of Malaysian Muslims—because it did not have the number of witnesses that their religion says is required.

On August 8, 2000. Anwar was found guilty of sodomy and sentenced to nine years in prison.

Even before the verdict was announced, Azizah expected that it would be guilty.

To many people, this was a political trial, and the verdict was pre-ordained. If that is true, then how can anyone say that this was a fair trial?

In a Malaysian court, there is only one judge, who is appointed by Mahathir, and there is no jury.

The nine years were added to Anwar's previous six-year sentence. So for the next fifteen years, until the year 2014, Anwar will be living in jail.

After the verdict was announced, the U.S. State Department said it was "outraged" by Anwar's conviction, which cast serious doubt on the impartiality and independence of Malaysia's judiciary.

The trial was condemned by legal groups around the world.

Vice President Al Gore, in the middle of his campaign for the U.S. Presidency, issued a statement saying he was "deeply disturbed" by the verdict. In strong language, he said, "The 'show trial' the two men were forced to endure mocked international standards of justice."

The International Bar Association in Geneva, the Asian Bar Association, and the Malaysian Bar Association issued statements one after another saying that the trial was unfair. The Governments of Canada and Australia also criticized the trial and verdict, as did the European Union. Major newspapers around the world, from Bangkok to Los Angeles, from Hong Kong to London, condemned what had happened.

It was regrettable that there was little reaction from Japan, whose businesses have always been close to Prime Minister Mahathir. Japan's newspapers barely reported the outcome. The articles I saw did not mention the fairness of the trial or Anwar's rights. Rather the focus was on what impact the verdict would have on the stock market and investment.

As a Japanese, I felt sad. Is Japan interested in nothing but business?

When I heard the verdict, I felt sad not just for Anwar and Azizah and their family. I felt sad that this kind of injustice could happen in the Malaysia that I knew.

The Malaysian people that I know are all good people. But has the situation in Malaysia now become so terrible that these good people are unable to do anything? How long will this situation continue?

When Anwar was Deputy Prime Minister, the Malaysian people were proud of him. Everyone had such high expectations. He would be a new leader not just for Malaysia, but also for Asia.

As an Asian and a Muslim, he could stand as an equal with the leaders of Europe and the United States and any other country. He could make a great contribution to Malaysia, Asia, and the whole world. He was the leader of the World Bank's Development Committee. Here was a political leader of great intellect and ability.

It is a great loss for Malaysia and the world that such a person should be away from us for 15 years. The greatest loss is not Anwar's or Azizah's. It is the Malaysian people and the people of all of Asia who have lost the most.

It is hard to believe that when Anwar opposed Mahathir, Mahathir could be so vengeful and cause this much pain!

Azizah and her family have been forced to go through a struggle that people in other countries cannot even imagine.

Two days after the verdict, Anwar celebrated his 52nd birthday in prison. And unless this injustice is reversed and he is freed, he will be in prison until he is 67.

Azizah has told the world, "Anwar's spirits are high." But I cannot help but wonder about the future. Can Anwar maintain his spirit for 15 years? But then I think of Mandela, who spent 27 years in prison.

And I think of the children, who are so precious to Azizah and Anwar. As a mother, Azizah knows that other children can say cruel things, and she wants to protect her children.

> "In school Hana was learning how to compose a question. So she wrote, "Where is my father?" Iman is nine years old, and after the verdict she asked her grandfather, "Is nine years a long time?" But on the birthday card that she sent to her Papa, she wrote "Long Live Anwar!"

After the second verdict, which was condemned as a travesty of justice by legal groups around the world, I spoke to Azizah on the telephone across those thousands of miles of ocean, and my heart went out to her.

What will happen from now on, I asked her?

> "Well, we will appeal Anwar's verdict, but I expect that it will be rejected just as it was the last time. But even when that happens, the Reformasi movement will not end. We are the ones who will carry on the torch that Anwar has lit. Anwar has sacrificed himself for reform and democracy in our country. From now on we are the ones who will carry on that struggle. Now we are the ones who must sacrifice."

Azizah hopes that information about what is happening in Malaysia will continue to spread throughout the world.

Now a "Free Anwar Campaign" has been established.

For myself, I am ready to provide whatever support I can, in the United States, in Japan, and anywhere, to support the movement to free Anwar. It is important for people all over the world to know what has happened to Anwar and to understand the situation in Malaysia.

Because we must never forget what Anwar said. "If it can happen to me, it can happen to anyone."

The Free Anwar Campaign is not just about releasing Anwar from prison. It is a crusade for human rights, for democracy, and for justice. It is a People's Crusade, to remind us that we are the ones who must protect our liberties and freedoms.

Our rights and our freedoms do not come from our rulers. They belong to us.

11

A Woman Called Azizah

Even in the midst of adversity,
the real Azizah shines through

A Woman Called Azizah

The first time I met Wan Azizah was a few months before my husband and I left America for his assignment in Malaysia. Deputy Prime Minister Anwar and his wife came to Washington on an official visit, and Anwar was making a speech at Johns Hopkins University.

It was the first time that I had met a Malaysian woman. Here was this small and slender person, wearing a shining silk *baju kurung*, the national dress of Malaysia. She covered her head with a pastel pink veil. Her face was beautiful, but I also could see a very intelligent and alert look to it. She moved and spoke quietly, as she walked a step behind her husband. Compared to the assertive behavior of other politicians' wives I have met over the years, I found her whole demeanor refreshing.

When she entered the room, I thought that I should stay my distance, but she sat down right next to me. So I summoned up the courage to say hello and speak to her in Malay, which I had been studying. She smiled and answered in Malay, and then she switched to perfect British English. She told me that she had six children, and that she was a medical doctor, with a specialty in ophthalmology.

After Anwar finished his speech, I told her that I thought it was brilliant. Azizah replied, "Thank you. You know, I'm his speechwriter." She smiled as she teased me. And then I realized that there was a difference between her "serious" appearance and her real personality. As time has gone on, I realized what a lively and witty person she is.

Azizah was born in the State of Kedah, which also is the home of Prime Minister Mahathir. When she was a young woman, Mahathir was a practicing physician in the city of Alor Setar. In an interview with *Aliran*, a Malaysian magazine, Azizah described her background:

> "I was born in Singapore and grew up in Kedah, Mahathir's state...Dr. Mahathir was a Member of Parliament when I was growing up. I remember Datin Seri Dr. Siti Hasmah (Mahathir's wife) came to officiate at my school's fun fair....And Marina Mahathir (Mahathir's daughter) was my junior in school.

"I studied in St. Nicholas Convent, in Alor Setar, from Standard One to Form Five. *(Editor's Note: for ten years).* I liked the Convent school very much. The nuns taught me a lot.

"I went to Tengku Kurshiah College for a while, and then I was in Dublin for six years. I was the top student for Obstetrics and Gynecology for my year and won a gold medal. My name is inscribed in the Hall of the College of Surgeons, which is very important because it is a Malaysian girl's name....But I don't usually brag, you know!"

After returning to Malaysia, Azizah did her internship at Kuala Lumpur's General Hospital. And it was there that she met her future husband, through another Mahathir connection of sorts:

"He was visiting Dr. Siti Hasmah's sister (Note: Mahathir's sister-in-law). She had appendicitis. I was on duty, and he came to see her, and that's how we met."

Because the Government had provided a scholarship for Azizah's medical studies in Ireland, she was obligated to work in the Government hospital for ten years.

"I did 14 years, until Anwar became Deputy Prime Minister. Then I stopped—and then I went back for volunteer service."

There was a third Mahathir connection in the personal lives of Azizah and Anwar. When they were married, Mahathir and his wife served as the official go-betweens for their wedding.

Throughout his political career, Anwar looked to Mahathir as a mentor and almost a father figure. It was Mahathir who brought Anwar into the ruling party, UMNO, when many others thought that Anwar would join the Islamic opposition party.

And now years later, they have become bitter political enemies.

The turning point was the Asian financial crisis of 1997. Anwar and Mahathir had very different approaches to dealing with the problem.

And it was about the same time that my friendship and admiration for Azizah grew.

The crisis affected the entire Asian region. In other countries, there were serious discussions about its causes, and how Government policies, corruption, and overborrowing and mismanagement by local companies were the causes. But in Malaysia, Mahathir decided to blame everything on America, the West, Wall Street, the IMF and others. He said that it was a plot to impoverish Malaysia and re-colonize it. America-bashing increased by the day.

Then one day the newspapers in Malaysia reported that Mahathir said that "the Jews" were behind the financial crisis. The reaction around the world was strong. Mahathir then denied that he said it, but the damage already had been done.

In Washington, some members of Congress called on Mahathir either to apologize, or resign. This demand only increased America-bashing in Malaysia, led by the Government and the press. Some American businessmen reported that angry Malaysians would confront them and tell them to "Go Home!"

Then the American Embassy received some threatening phone calls. The callers said that they were going to kill Americans in Malaysia. The Embassy was required to inform the American community of these threats, and it did so. But this only made Mahathir and his supporters angrier. They thought we were trying to scare American investment away from Malaysia during a financial crisis.

Tensions reached an all-time high. So my husband called an emergency press conference. He stressed the importance of US-Malaysia relations, and then he called on both sides to calm the rhetoric and "cool it." He said that Malaysia should stop its "America-bashing." As for the US Congressmen, he put his job at risk by saying that it was inappropriate of them to call upon the democratically-elected leader of another country to resign.

While the Malaysians were both pleased and surprised that he criticized his own Congressmen, there was silence about his call to end the dangerous America-bashing in Malaysia.

Everyone knew that although his language was very careful and diplomatic, his message to "cool it" was directed at Mahathir.

The next day I was invited to a meeting held by a charity group, where Azizah would be the speaker. I was the only foreigner there. The Malaysians who knew me hesitated to talk to me, because they did not know what they should say. In Malaysia, many people wait to hear what Mahathir has to say first, and then they follow his guidance.

Azizah then entered the hall, followed by the wives of a number of Cabinet Ministers. She shook hands with some people in the audience, and then she saw me. She walked over to me and said, "Mrs. Malott, thank you for coming," and she put her hand on my shoulder very lightly. "I saw Ambassador Malott's press conference on television last night. Your husband was very courageous, and please let him know I said so."

When her speech was over and it was time for her to leave, she came up to me again and said, "Please come with me to have some tea." She took my hand and led me to the VIP room. The change in attitude among everyone in the room was very noticeable when she did that.

I had felt alone until that point, but she handled the whole situation in such a natural way. She protected me at a difficult time, and she did it publicly. Others did not know what to think or say before, but Azizah courageously sent a signal to them. Not only did she encourage me personally, she sent a political message as well.[1]

One year later, the tables were turned. Now it was my turn to summon up the courage to support her.

---

1. Anwar did the same thing for my husband a day later. In full view of the Malaysian press, he walked over to my husband at a gathering and struck up a conversation. The TV and newspaper photographers rushed to take pictures. Their conversation was purely social, but the public political message was the same one that Azizah sent—America is an important country to Malaysia, and the bashing should stop.

   As for Mahathir, my husband says that after his press conference calling for an end to the attacks on America, Mahathir never spoke to him again. In fact, Mahathir would try to avoid looking at him at public gatherings during the final year of his assignment in Malaysia.

12

Azizah's Future, Malaysia's Future

Azizah applauds as she launches her new political party

AZIZAH'S FUTURE, MALAYSIA'S FUTURE

Oh, Malaysia!

What a beautiful country it is.

And what wonderful people.

How much we enjoyed the first part of our assignment there, before the country was thrown into economic and political crisis.

It is a country of so many strengths. It has made great economic progress since its independence in 1957.

Its people comes from so many cultural and religious backgrounds, and yet they live together in harmony and mutual respect. No matter what their race or religion, they all are proud of being Malaysians.

Malaysians are a very friendly and open people. They are fun-loving and fun to be around. Perhaps nothing symbolizes this more than the tradition of "Open Houses." At the Muslim New Year, Eid'il Fitri, everyone from the Prime Minister on down opens their homes to receive visitors. Anyone who wants to come is welcome to do so. They exchange New Year's greetings, and the host provides his guests with refreshments.

The Prime Minister would stand patiently in line, with no security guards around him, to welcome over 10,000 people to his Residence. There were not just Malaysians of all races—even foreign tourists would come to say hello.

During my 30 years as the wife of an American diplomat, I have traveled to so many lands. But Malaysia is one of the most fascinating and pleasant countries on earth.

And that is why I was so sad as I wrote this book. It is not the story that I wanted to tell. I wanted to talk about the other Malaysia.

But that was not to be. As someone who has been a citizen and lived most of her life in two great democracies, Japan and the United States, I believe that freedom and our rights as human beings matter. When other people are deprived of the freedoms that we take for granted, it is wrong.

What has happened in that wonderful country of Malaysia is not right, and I cannot remain silent. A great injustice has been done, but not just to Anwar, Azizah, and their family. It has happened to all the people of Malaysia.

When I left Kuala Lumpur at the end of 1998, I promised Azizah that I would tell people in Japan what was going on in Malaysia. Little did I know that it would turn into a book about Azizah herself, and that it would be available in both Japanese and English.

Azizah, I have kept my promise to you. I have tried to tell the world about what has happened.

So as I end my book, what I can say to you now?

I don't want to tell you that you should be strong, because you have been so strong for such a long time—for Anwar and your family, and for so many others in Malaysia who believe in freedom and justice.

They gave you the torch to carry. It is not something you asked for. But you have become their hope. You are the symbol of justice in Malaysia. You have become the sunlight not only for your family but for so many others as well. And I know that they give you the courage and the reason to go on.

Do you remember when you explained why you can still smile and carry on, no matter how difficult your days have been?

You quoted the Koran and said God does not give you a burden greater than what you can bear. You said that you are sure that there is wisdom in everything that happens. And you said that as a Muslim, you believe that in the end God will reward those who do right, and that justice will prevail.

I don't know how long God will test you and make you carry this burden. But like you, I believe that in the end, justice will prevail.

13

Update 2002:
The Struggle Continues

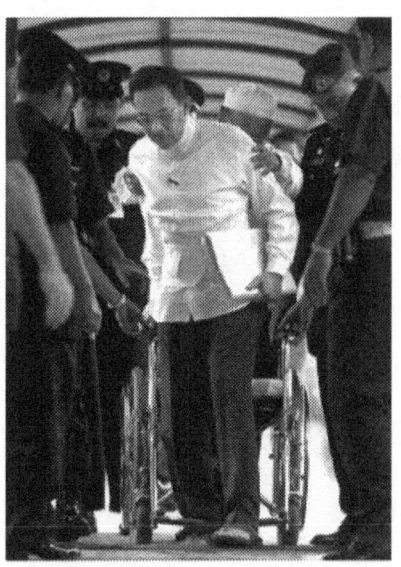

Suffering from a prolapsed disc and other ailments,
Anwar has to be helped to stand

Update 2002:
The Struggle Continues

It has been over one year since I wrote my book in Japanese for the internet website *La Vie en Rose*.

And it has been nearly four years since Wan Azizah's nightmare began—when her husband, the second most powerful man in Malaysia, was taken away at gunpoint.

The Japanese version of my book tells the story of what happened in the two years after that fateful night.

What has happened in the two years since I wrote my book for the Japanese internet? That is the subject of this chapter, which I have written for this English translation.

We always hope for a happy ending—whether it is a children's story or a Hollywood movie.

But in this case, there still is no happy ending.

Anwar has been in jail for over three years. He has 14 years left on his sentence.

Now Anwar is suffering from a prolapsed disc. He can barely walk, and if surgery is not performed, he may end up paralyzed.

Yet the Malaysian Government has not allowed him to get the latest medical treatment. He wants to go to Germany to undergo endoscopic surgery by one of the world's leading surgeons, Dr. Thomas Hoog, but the Government has refused.

Two years before, Prime Minister Mahathir said that maybe Anwar had beaten himself up. This time Mahathir said that maybe Anwar was "faking" his back injury.

Then, after the Government's own doctors released their medical reports confirming Anwar's medical problems, Mahathir said that if Anwar goes to Germany, he will never come back.

But Anwar knows that if he stays overseas, it is "political suicide" in Malaysia. He will lose support among the Malaysian people.

So Anwar offered to go to Germany under Malaysian police escort to ensure his return to his homeland. And still the Government refused.

They told him that he must undergo surgery in Malaysia, using much older technology, with doctors from the Government's hospital—or he would be sent back to prison. He would not be allowed to choose his own doctors.

After all that has happened to him—including being beaten nearly to death by the Government's head of police—it is easy to understand why Anwar hesitated and why he could not trust his own Government.

Anwar showed his courage once again. If that is my choice, he said, I will go back to prison. And that is where he is today.

His condition continues to worsen, adding to Azizah's worries.

Meanwhile, the Government's crackdown on the political opposition has gotten worse. Harun Rashid, a highly respected Malaysian intellectual, has written that:

> "There is no freedom of the press. The press is owned and controlled by the (Government) parties and no dissent is allowed....The media has lost such public respect that few newspapers or TV stations can operate at a profit.

> "The public, seeking truth, has moved to high technology for its news and communication. Computers and the Internet are favored.

> "Recognizing this trend, the official policy is to interfere wherever possible, sending viruses to opposition writers and opposition discussion groups. Many in the secret police are employed to act as propaganda agents, fomenting dissent and disseminating fabrications.

"A favored means of the opposition to present news and talks by popular personalities is through VCDs distributed rapidly throughout the country. Now the party in power, under the pretext of 'fighting piracy', is propagating a policy of prohibiting sale of VCDs by the many street vendors."

But the Government is not just cracking down on the internet and videos and VCDs. It also has been arresting many of Anwar's supporters under the sedition laws and the Internal Security Act.

The Government has targeted a number of leaders of Azizah's Keadilan Party and the Free Anwar movement.

The first one arrested was Mohamed Ezam, the leader of Keadilan's youth movement. The Government charged that when he was abroad, Ezam said that foreign companies should not invest in Malaysia because of the political situation.

The Government arrested him under its sedition law. But where did the Government get its information about what Ezam said? From an article in a Malaysian newspaper called *Utusan*.

Is everything you read in the newspapers anywhere in the world true? Or should you investigate it first, before you arrest someone?

Let me tell you this story about my husband and that same newspaper, *Utusan*.

One morning a few months ago we were sitting in our California home, drinking our morning coffee. My husband went to the computer, just like he always does, and checked the news from around the world.

He screamed and said, "Hiroko! Did you know I was in Malaysia yesterday? It must have been my clone who was here with you!"

That very same newspaper, *Utusan*, reported in its top story on the front page that my husband had been in Malaysia, attending a "secret meeting" with Azizah and her party.

And now the same newspaper was making a statement that might lead to Ezam spending the rest of his life in jail.

After Ezam was arrested, a few of his friends went to the police station to hold a candlelight vigil

They were arrested, too!

Two of them were friends of ours—but friends we know only through email. They are friends who also believe in freedom—Raja Petra Kamaruddin and his courageous wife, Marina.

We have never met them in person. But Raja—who is the nephew of the King of Malaysia—is one of the leaders of the worldwide Free Anwar Campaign.

Why were they arrested, simply for holding candles? Because it is illegal for more than four people to gather in Malaysia without police permission.

So they held a candle, and they spent the night in jail.

One day later, Raja and his wife were released. Raja then sent an eloquent email to his many friends around the world:

> "My wife and I thank you for the concern and kind words expressed.
>
> "When I was sitting on the dirty floor in the smelly police lockup, which became my accommodation for the night, I asked myself, what am I doing here? Is it worth all the trouble?
>
> "When the police told me they are investigating me for sedition and I could go to jail for a long time, my heart sank. It's so easy to shout slogans with arms raised and fists punching the air in a crowd of supporters. But when you are all alone, arms handcuffed behind your back, and being questioned by one police officer after another, it is so hard not to break.
>
> "They wanted names, but I kept replying, "I refuse to answer on the grounds that I have promised to protect their identities." They asked me why go down alone when I can make it easier on myself. At that point it

is so tempting to just tell them what they wanted to know and relieve yourself of the burden of taking the rap.

"When I agreed to head the Free Anwar Campaign it was a political thing. I never in a million years imagined what Anwar was really going through. I spend one night in a lockup with the prospect of only three years jail and I feel my life has changed. Imagine Anwar's feeling knowing he has 13 years to go and the prospect of another five [trials and] sentences to come.

"Freedom is the most valuable thing we possess. We lose that and it's worse than losing life itself. Everything in this world minus freedom is worthless.

"I now know what I am fighting for. Life without freedom means nothing. And freedom can never be yours under an oppressive and corrupt government. And that's why we need change and reformation."

Raja continued his work for the Free Anwar Campaign, as the director of its website (*www.freeanwar.com*).

But then, on April 11 the Government cracked down again. Raja and other supporters of Anwar and Azizah were arrested under the dreadful Internal Security Act, just as Anwar had been.

Now the struggle for justice spread to other wives and families. Now others would not know where their husbands, sons and fathers, and fiancés were.

This time it was Raja's courageous wife Marina who stepped forward to demand the right to see her husband. As one wife to another, she wrote to Dr. Siti Hasmah, the wife of the Prime Minister:

"I am the wife of Raja Petra Kamaruddin, and I am writing to Datin Seri on behalf of all wives and family members of the seven ISA detainees who would like to appeal to [you] to persuade the Prime Minister to allow us to visit our husbands.

"Our children and we have had terrible nightmares thinking of them and their health. We cannot believe that in a developed country like Malaysia [that is] already in the 21st century, we are faced with situation like this.

"Our husbands are not being kidnapped by terrorists but…by our own government.…We do not know whether our husbands have been beaten or castigated while in detention. Have they received proper meals or the right medication?

"What has happened to Dato' Seri Anwar Ibrahim [while in custody] has brought us to have minimal trust of the police.

"We have grounds in our feelings and I once again appeal to Datin Seri to deliver this matter to your husband to consider on these humanitarian grounds."

Ezam's three children, aged 8, 4, and 3, also wrote a letter pleading for their father's release:

"We want to see our father. He is a good man. We hope you will release our father and Anwar."

Raja eventually was released, and he wrote a book about his ordeal, called *From Prince to Prisoner*. To the surprise of many, three other prisoners were released by a courageous judge who said that the Government had failed to prove its charges that the arrestees were a threat to national security.

But as for Ezam and other leaders in Azizah's party, they were sent away to prison for two years as threats to the nation's security. They were never brought to trial, evidence was never produced, and they were never seen in public again after their arrest. The Government never has had to prove its accusations against them.[1]

They simply were locked up.

What has happened in the Malaysia that I love so much?

---

1.   After serving two years detention without trial, Ezam has now been released.

14

Justice Prevails

Immediately after his release, Anwar and Azizah
hold a press conference at their home.
That is Azizah's biggest smile in six years.

JUSTICE PREVAILS

It is September 2, 2004.

It is six years since Azizah's husband Anwar was first thrown in jail. Six years since Azizah's struggle for justice began. All of the court cases, the legal maneuverings, the appeals, the international pressure—until now, everything has come to the same dead end.

And today, September 2, is Anwar's last chance.

Malaysia's Federal Court—similar to the Supreme Court in the United States[1]—will render its decision on Anwar's appeal against the verdict that found him guilty of sodomy.

If Anwar loses again, it means he will spend another nine years in prison. Even if he gets time off for good behavior, he will not be a free man for at least six more years. For Anwar, it will make a political comeback next to impossible. In Malaysia, the Government and the press have been telling everyone that Anwar is a forgotten man, and that his Reformasi movement is a spent force. In the most recent Parliamentary elections, Azizah was the only member of her Keadilan Party to win reelection.

For the children, it will mean more years without their Papa. Hana, only six years old when her father was carried off into the night by the masked SWAT team, will be a university student when her father is freed. In the past six years, Anwar was let out of prison only twice—once to attend his mother's funeral, and the second time, for just two hours, to be at his eldest daughter Izzah's wedding[2]

For Azizah, it will mean more years of a burden that most people could never face.

---

1. Except that there are three justices, not nine
2. Even though the Government claimed that Anwar was forgotten, over 30,000 people showed up for Azizah's wedding reception when it was held in Anwar's former political constituency.

But the greatest concern for everyone in September 2004 was Anwar's deteriorating medical condition. The pain from his slipped disc was unbearable. He was immobile. He had to be helped to stand, and to go from place to place he needed a wheel chair. Anwar still refused to undergo surgery in Malaysia, where medical technology—especially in the prison hospital—lagged behind that of Germany, the United States, and elsewhere. If Anwar were not freed, and if he continued to refuse treatment in Malaysia, he might end up paralyzed.

In America, with the time change it was the evening of September 1, and my husband John and I had just finished celebrating my birthday. We called Azizah. As it turned out, she already was on her way to court, so we reached her on her cellphone.

John asked her how it looked. Prime Minister Mahathir—the man who sacked Anwar from office and threw him in jail—had retired, and there was hope that under the new Prime Minister, Abdullah Ahmad Badawi, things might be better. Azizah said, "I've been getting good vibes, but I don't want to get my hopes up. We've been disappointed so many times."

John said that he had heard the same thing. The rumor mill in Kuala Lumpur was in full swing. The word was that in their internal meeting, the three judges had voted 2-1 to overturn the lower court decision and free Anwar—but the rumors also said that some in the Government were putting strong pressure on one of the two judges to change his vote.

Even in the middle of this discussion, with everything that was on her mind, Azizah remembered that it was my birthday. It was just one year earlier that she had been in Washington DC and joined in my birthday dinner. She wished me a Happy Birthday and said that she was sorry she had not sent a present. "All I want for my birthday is for Anwar to be free," I said. "That will be the best present of all."

After the phone call, we waited a very long 90 minutes. John knew that the fastest way to learn the verdict would be over the internet. There were two websites in Malaysia—*Malaysiakini* and *Free Anwar*—that would probably broadcast the verdict immediately.

As the Chief Justice read out the verdict, a *Malaysiakini* reporter in the courtroom tapped out an email message on his cellphone, and within a minute it was uploaded onto the website and sent around the world on the internet.

Half a world away we read what we had been waiting for. Six years of waiting, and what we saw was just six words:

"Flash! Anwar Freed! Details to follow."

We called Azizah immediately. There was pandemonium at the other end of the phone line. Everyone was shouting in the background, and we could barely hear Azizah's soft but excited voice. "Anwar is free! The verdict was overturned!" Then she said, "Just a minute," and the next voice we heard was Anwar's. "Hello. How are you?" he said.

We knew that Anwar was surrounded by his family and friends, who all wanted a word with him, so we said we would call later. He gave the phone back to Azizah. I told her how much I admired her. "You never gave up, Azizah."

John and I looked at each other and did not know what to think. I was numb. After a six year struggle, it was over, just like that. It took only one man, one judge, in a 2-1 vote. He could have changed his mind and decided the other way—and Anwar would still be in jail. But tonight Anwar would be sleeping in his own house, in his own bed, for the first time in six years. Instead of spending his days in solitary confinement, he would be surrounded once again by the people who loved him most.

In the days that followed, thousands of people came to Anwar's home. From morning to night, everyone wanted to see the man that the Government claimed was "forgotten." Journalists lined up to interview him.

For six years, only relatives and the closest of friends came to visit, but now Anwar's once-quiet house in Bukit Damansara was like the center of a giant street festival. Enterprising hawkers (street vendors) set up refreshment stands to serve the crowds. The excitement and visitors were so great that one of Anwar's daughters, Ilham, said on the phone, "Auntie Hiroko, it's just like the old days!"

Two days after Anwar's release, we called Azizah, and Anwar asked to speak to both John and me. He thanked us for all of the support that we had given to him and his family. For our part, we told him what a great family he has. Who wouldn't want to stand by such wonderful people?

Now that he was free, Anwar also was free to make his own medical decisions. He made plans to go to Munich, Germany to a spinal clinic that specializes in non-invasive laser surgery. When he and Azizah departed from Kuala Lumpur's international airport, over 10,000 people came to see them off.

On Saturday, September 11, the phone rang. It was Azizah calling from Munich, telling me that Anwar's surgery was a tremendous success. In fact, with some assistance Anwar had walked back to his room.

It was hard to believe. In less than ten days, Azizah's world had turned around with two great miracles. Her husband was freed, and now his spinal problem was cured. I had never heard Azizah sound so happy.

Her struggle for justice was over.

Afterword
By the Author

The author and Dr. Wan Azizah Wan Ismail
visit with each other in Washington, DC in February 2005,
following Anwar's release from prison and successful surgery

AFTERWORD
BY THE AUTHOR

Dear Azizah,

At last your struggle is over.

During all those years, you never gave up hope.

You still could smile and carry on, no matter how difficult those days and years were.

You kept your strength for your husband and your family, and for so many others in Malaysia who believe in freedom and justice.

I shall always treasure our friendship, and I feel fortunate that my life crossed yours.

Azizah, you are truly an amazing and wonderful person. I shall always remember what you said:

> "There is wisdom in everything that happens.
>
> "And in the end, God will reward those who do right, and justice will prevail."

Afterword
by Anwar Ibrahim

Afterword
by Anwar Ibrahim

We had known Hiroko as the wife of John Malott, the US ambassador to Malaysia when I was deputy prime minister of Malaysia. Hiroko came to know Azizah through various official functions. Little did we know that our formal acquaintance would blossom into such close friendship.

When I was sacked from the government and later incarcerated, many fair weathered friends abandoned us. But what encouraged me during the trying years was that we gained unexpected new friends. They are our genuine friends. John and Hiroko are in this category, particularly after John's retirement as ambassador and the couple taking up residence in Washington. And my children also became very close to them, happy to address them as 'Uncle John' and 'Auntie Hiroko.'

This book compiled by Hiroko is a result of her labor of love and her personal tribute to Azizah. I suppose such tribute can only come from a woman, because only a woman can fully sympathize, appreciate and empathize with the depths of sacrifice made and demanded of my wife. The burden of politics, continuing the *reformasi* movement and founding a new party was thrust upon her with such suddenness and utter unpreparedness. She had to face harassment from the authorities, a barrage of adverse media propaganda, and overwhelming political and familial responsibilities. Amidst such difficulties I believe Azizah's spirit was often lifted by encouraging words from friends like Hiroko.

However, Hiroko's role is more than extending personal sympathy. She was also an effective campaigner for our cause in Japan. Because of the pervasive collusion of Malaysia-Japan business interests, the mainstream media in Japan tended to be less sympathetic. Hiroko was instrumental in improving media coverage for us in Japan. Through her contacts she arranged the visit of our daughter Nurul Izzah where she articulated the justice of our cause to the Japanese public.

We extend our deepest gratitude to sincere and genuine friends, who stood by us through a difficult period. To John and Hiroko, your kindness and support will be forever imprinted in our hearts and living memory.

Anwar Ibrahim

978-0-595-37586-8
0-595-37586-3